Pumpkn's Secret

D. L. STENGER

Illustrations BY KATHY BURNS

AuthorHouse™
1663 Liberty Drive
Bloomington, IN 47403
www.authorhouse.com
Phone: 833-262-8899

Because of the dynamic nature of the Internet, any web addresses or links contained in this book may have changed
since publication and may no longer be valid. The views expressed in this work are solely those of the author and do not
necessarily reflect the views of the publisher, and the publisher hereby disclaims any responsibility for them.

Any people depicted in stock imagery provided by Getty Images are models,
and such images are being used for illustrative purposes only.
Certain stock imagery © Getty Images.

This book is printed on acid-free paper.

ISBN: 978-1-4259-5055-2 (sc)
ISBN: 978-1-4634-5408-1 (e)

Library of Congress Control Number: 2006906330

Print information available on the last page.

Published by AuthorHouse 06/08/2022

authorHOUSE®

I would like to take this opportunity to give glory to Almighty God the Father, Who has been my constant strength and to Jesus Christ, my Savior during all those years of living through my abusive childhood. He has always had a plan for me, continually guiding and inspiring me through the Holy Spirit, bringing me to this point in my life where He can now use me to help others heal who must live the sad reality of domestic violence.

DEDICATION

This book is dedicated to all of the children whose souls have been stained by endless suffering in an environment plagued with domestic violence.

ACKNOWLEDGEMENTS

I would like to give special thanks to Daryl "Sonny" Stenger, Samuel L. Obenschain, Nancy Delf, Christie Shapiro, Lynn Hineman, H.K. Rickenbaker III, Linda Sussman, MS, Denise Olive, LLC, MS, Licensed Professional Counselor and Dr. Ade Donsunmu, M.D., Medical Director of SuperHero Clinics in Hinesville, Georgia. Most of all, I would like to thank my son Vinny for understanding I have always been a work in progress because of my upbringing. Thank you for all your support in the early stages.

This is the story of a little girl named Pumpkn who has a **BIG** secret. At the time of this story, Pumpkn was ten years old and had a little brother who was six named Bobby. Although she felt sad most of the time, she did find moments of happiness here and there. She really enjoyed spending time alone playing with some of her favorite toys. This gave her time to think about her feelings. ***What are some of your favorite toys?***

Pumpkn went to school every day just like you do. Her favorite teacher was also her homeroom teacher. Pumpkn's homeroom was room #108. She loved Mrs. Gano because she smelled very nice and was always very, very kind to Pumpkn—maybe she suspected what her secret was! ***Who is your favorite teacher? Do you think you know Pumpkn's secret?***

Even though Pumpkn loved her teacher, she couldn't seem to focus and concentrate like all the other children. She just couldn't keep up and thought she was stupid. That meant she never raised her hand or participated in class. Unfortunately, her homework was never finished on time. Thank goodness her close friend Gracie would help with her schoolwork when she fell behind. *Why do think Pumpkn had problems in school?*

During English class, all of the students got their tests back that they had taken the day before. When Pumpkn got hers back, it had a big red *"F"* on the top. She was sad and very embarrassed, ***especially*** when some of the other classmates saw it. The little girl with the freckles yelled, "Look! Pumpkn got an *F*! She probably didn't study again!" Pumpkn remembered why she couldn't study and became angry. ***Do you know why she couldn't study?***

Well, the reason that Pumpkn couldn't study the night before was because she was worried about her safety and the safety of her little brother, Bobby. She tried to find a place that would be big enough for both of them to hide in, so she emptied out one of the kitchen cabinets and put all of the pots and pans into a smaller cabinet. Bobby played with some of the pots like they were drums. Pumpkn had a tummy full of "bad butterfiles." She didn't like that feeling, but she had it a lot. *NOW **do you think you know Pumpkn's secret?***

After English class it was time to go to lunch. Pumpkn put her bad grades behind her and walked down the hall with Gracie to the lunchroom. They went to lunch together every day. Pumpkn didn't have a lot of friends and kept to herself most of the time, but this friend was special. Gracie always got good grades and she liked to make Pumpkn laugh. Pumpkn wanted to be just like her. ***Do you have a friend to look up to?***

She remembered the good time that she had over the weekend at Gracie's house. Gracie's mom had made a spaghetti dinner just for the two of them. Afterwards, they went up to Gracie's room and ate Doritos and played the game of Life. Pumpkn loved the warm, homey feeling she got when she was at Gracie's house. ***Do you like spaghetti?***

Pumpkn was having so much fun laughing with Gracie walking to the cafeteria, she forgot that she didn't have any lunch. Pumpkn's mom was angry that morning and woke up late to take her to school. When Pumpkn reminded her mom that she forgot to pack her a lunch, her mom just snapped, "Go *borrow* money from someone."

As Pumpkn was walking out of the kitchen to get into the car, she saw a box of Hostess Ho-Ho's on the counter. She quickly grabbed one and put it in her book bag. That would be her lunch that day. At the lunch table some of the other kids asked where the rest of her lunch was. "Is that all that you brought today?" Pumpkn was so sad that she felt like crying, but she stayed strong. ***Do you know what to do if you don't have any lunch or lunch money?***

Just then, Stephanie sat down next to her and offered Pumpkn some of her lunch. Stephanie felt sorry for Pumpkn because this wasn't the first time that she saw her friend without something to eat. "Is everything okay? Don't feel bad; sometimes I forget my lunch too." Stephanie tried to make Pumpkn feel better but deep down she knew that Pumpkn had some kind of problem that she wasn't telling her. *You still don't know what her secret is?*

Embarrassed for the second time that day, Pumpkn sat at the lunchroom table and began daydreaming of what it might be like to have a real family. Again, she thought of Gracie and her mom. She wished that she could live with them and be part of their family. Pumpkn daydreamed *a lot*—sometimes it helped her just to get through the day. ***Have you ever daydreamed?***

On the way to her next class, Pumpkn passed the chapel on the school grounds. She would frequently stop in during the day because it always gave her a peaceful feeling. The colorful stained glass windows sparkled beautifully when the bright sun would shine down through them. It was the perfect place to go when she was having a hard day. ***What do you do when you have a hard day?***

Pumpkn prayed: "Dear God, I know you're busy but I really need your help. Please help me to be a better student. I try so hard but nothing seems to work out right. I know I can count on you. And P.S.—please don't let my mommy and daddy fight again tonight. Amen." After praying, Pumpkn went to her history class.

It was the last class of the day and almost time to go home. "Psssssst, Pumpkn." Gracie was trying to get Pumpkn's attention to tell her that she wouldn't be able to wait with her after school. She had to go to band rehearsal and then basketball practice after that. Gracie was very involved in school programs. Pumpkn didn't participate in school activities. *Do you think that is good or bad?*

Someone seemed a little nervous—it was Pumpkn. She was chewing on her pencil and twirling her hair, constantly watching the clock. It was the end of a long day for this little girl, but unfortunately, it was far from over. She was nervous because she knew if her mother's car wasn't outside in the parking lot when she got out of school, she simply wasn't coming.

It was just as Pumpkn had feared—her mom wasn't there. This had happened many times before...more times than she could count. Pumpkn was afraid to be outside the school all by herself, but she knew what she had to do. She waited for about five more minutes and then went back inside.

What would you do if you were the last one at school? Always remember to be safe and never, EVER accept a ride with strangers. You should do what Pumpkn is going to do—go straight to the office and report to a teacher that you don't have a ride.

Pumpkn kept her chin up and went to the school office to get permission to use the phone so she could call home. She was just thankful that there were adults still at the school because she didn't want to be alone. After the third phone call, her mom finally answered and told her that she was on the way. The school secretary checked to make sure that someone was coming to get her, and feeling relieved, Pumpkn thanked her.

Going home! Finally! What a long day! Pumpkn couldn't wait to get home and change into her comfy clothes and watch her favorite television show—***The Munsters. What's your favorite television show?***

After Pumpkn and Bobby enjoyed an after-school snack, they went into the family room. Pumpkn read the comics while Bobby played with some blocks. Their mother was in her sewing room making a prom dress for the neighbor's daughter—she was a very good seamstress. In fact, she looks just like every other mom, doesn't she?

When their father got home, he sat quietly reading the paper. Even though things seemed quiet on the home front, Pumpkn's tummy sensed that something just wasn't right—but she couldn't put her finger on it. He seems just like any other dad, doesn't he? So she took her little brother and went up to her room before it was time for dinner.

Pumpkn was reading her favorite Christmas stories to Bobby when she heard yelling and screaming coming from the stairs. *Here we go again*, she thought. She was almost sure that her mom and dad had seemed calm when she left to come upstairs. After hearing the yelling again, she told Bobby to stay put and went to investigate.

She quietly crept halfway down the stairs so she could hear what was going on. **CRASH! BANG!** Was that a dish breaking? She had to get closer. Pumpkn could hear her own heart beating loudly in her ears and her tummy was one big knot. Her intuition was right! **SLAP!**

As scared as she was, she decided to get *even closer! Is this a smart thing to do?*

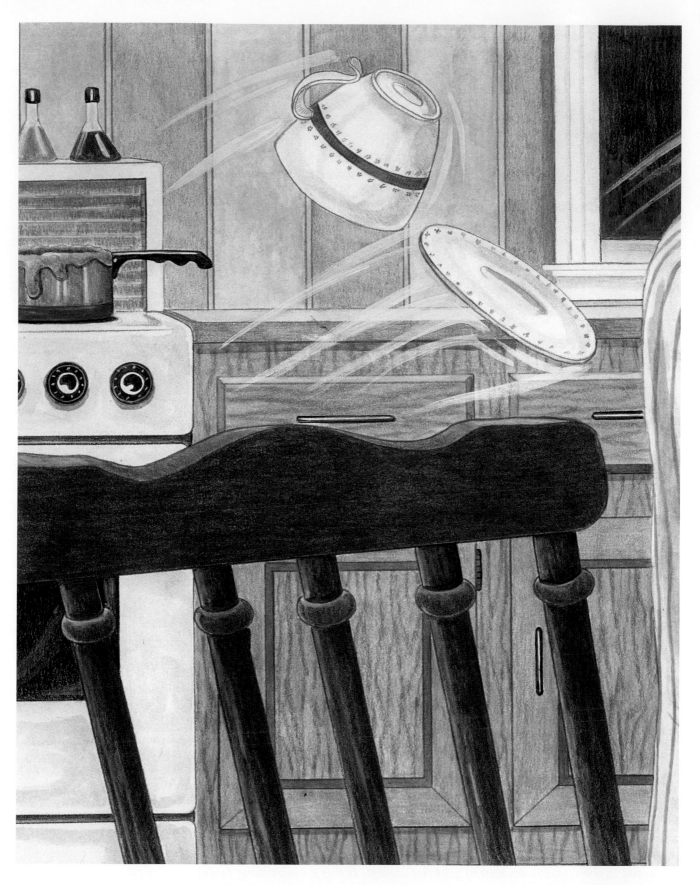

This is Pumpkn's secret. She lives in a home with parents who fight. She lives in a home with **domestic violence**. Dishes breaking and her mommy and daddy screaming and yelling are ordinary circumstances in Pumpkn's life. This is why she can't concentrate on her schoolwork. This is why Pumpkn looks for places to hide and protect her little brother. **Do you know anyone who lives with domestic violence?**

As she turned the corner into the kitchen, a cup and saucer flew across the room, almost hitting her right in the head. *Whoa!* she thought. *That was a close one!* Pumpkn was in danger, and it was time to do something—*anything*. She wondered if her little brother had stayed where she told him to. Even though she stepped into the danger zone she never forgot about Bobby's safety.

Think! Think! I have to make them stop! I can do it! Pumpkn was so tired of all of the violence in her home night after night. She would make believe that one day a superhero like Batman or Spider Man would come charging in to save the day and make her parents quit fighting. Maybe if she had magic powers she could make it all go away, but deep down she knew that could never happen. She couldn't take any more, and decided to go stop the violence herself. ***Do you think it is a good idea that Pumpkn tries to do this on her own?***

This could have been a HUGE mistake! "Stop it, Mommy, Daddy!" They were so busy fighting that they didn't even notice Pumpkn was there. She tried yelling and screaming at them to stop. She even jumped in between them and tried to push them apart, but they just kept on fighting and even pushed her out of the way. Once Pumpkn realized they weren't going to listen, she ran to check on her little brother and then called her Aunt Peaches. ***Should Pumpkn have put herself in danger?***

Pumpkn loved her Aunt Peaches. She was loving, calm and always knew what to do—plus she knew about the fighting between her mom and dad and understood Pumpkn's feelings. She ran to her parents' bedroom to make the call so they wouldn't hear her. The phone rang and rang. She was afraid that her aunt might not be home. ***Do you have someone like Aunt Peaches that you can call if you are in danger?***

Aunt Peaches finally answered the phone and said, "Hello sweetheart. Calm down, calm down. Everything's going to be fine. Do you remember what I told you? If you don't feel safe, go get Bobby and go to the neighbor's house. Don't forget to call me when you get there so I know you're okay. And don't forget that I love you!" Pumpkn immediately started calming down just like she always did when she talked to her Aunt Peaches.

So Pumpkn grabbed Bobby, some extra clothes and her clipboard. She always made notes on her clipboard and never went anywhere without it. Still dressed in their pajamas, they ran outside their house and underneath the kitchen window. "Where are we going?" asked Bobby. "It's going to be okay. We're just going to the neighbor's house until things quiet down…trust me."

The neighbor, Miss Lil, also knew about Pumpkn's family situation. They were just in time for freshly baked warm cookies and a nice cold glass of milk. They were finally safe. Miss Lil gave them a hug and told them not to worry. She promised that she would take care of everything. Pumpkn was relieved to be able to calm down after all of the action she had had to deal with. She made sure that she called Aunt Peaches to let her know they were safe. ***Do you have somewhere to go if you're in the same situation as Pumpkn?***

By the time Miss Lil called Pumpkn's parents, the fighting was over. Do you know that they didn't even realize that Pumpkn and her little brother had gone? Pumpkn's dad assured Miss Lil that it was safe to bring them home, and it was. Bobby seemed unsure, but he trusted his big sister.

Her dad told her not to worry and that it would never happen again. But she had heard these promises many times before. He also said that he didn't *want* to hit her mom, but that she *made* him do it. Pumpkn didn't believe him—not even for *one second*! She knew she still had to be careful for her and her brother's safety.

Finally upstairs and ready for bed, Pumpkn and Bobby said their prayers—it had been a long day! Pumpkn was very thankful for all of those who had helped her get through the day: God, Gracie, Stephanie, the school secretary, Aunt Peaches and Miss Lil. She was tired and so was Bobby. They were ready for bed.

Right before bed, Pumpkn stared into her bedroom mirror reflecting on her chaotic day and was proud that she had been able to keep herself and her brother safe and handle all of the challenges that came her way. She thought of all the children out in the world who were going through the same thing, maybe even **worse** things than she had to live with. She promised herself that one day she would help them.

SAFETY TIPS

Follow-up Topics for Class Discussion

1. **Don't be afraid to spend time alone.** Use this time to relax. Think about how you're feeling and how you might prepare yourself for possible trouble. Use that time for coloring or building puzzles or Legos... things that take your mind off your anxiety.

2. **Don't feel like you're a failure.** Because you are not! You must remember: you are not responsible for what is going on in your home. The violence in your home is a distraction to your concentration and you will have many opportunities to shine and do your best.

3. **It is *NOT* your fault they are fighting.** It is also not your responsibility to stop the fighting. It *is* your responsibility to stay safe.

SAFETY & SELF ESTEEM GO HAND IN HAND!

4. **Find a "safe place" to hide** until the fighting is over—a closet, a cabinet or maybe behind a chair in another room. Don't forget about your siblings.

5. **Always tell your teacher if you don't have any lunch money.** You need to eat to keep up your strength and to keep your mind sharp. There are programs in the school to help with this. And no one else needs to know.

6. **Don't ever just walk home if you're left at school.** Make sure that you tell a teacher that your mom or dad is not outside and that you might not have a way home. Let the teacher decide the best way to handle the situation.

7. **Listen to your tummy!** When you're hungry your tummy lets you know it by growling, and when you're in danger your tummy will also let you know by giving you "bad butterflies." Learn to trust your instincts—they may save your life one day.

8. **Never get between fighting parents. Period!** If they argue in front of you they will not be aware of your safety and you could get seriously injured. Stay out of the danger zone!

9. **Have someone you can call when a fight breaks out.** Maybe it's your aunt or uncle or your grandmother or a neighbor. Try to stay calm so you can think clearly.

10. **Pick out a neighbor's house**—some place close, in advance. You might have to run for help if you feel you are in any serious danger, especially if you see any knives, guns or anything that might be used as a weapon. Don't be afraid to tell your neighbor about the violence...you will probably keep your parents from getting hurt.

11. **Always stay alert!** If your mommy and daddy have fought before it will probably happen again, and you want to be ready.

12. **Understand that you are living in a situation that is serious and could be very dangerous.** You are learning valuable life survival skills that could help you be a great leader some day. By thinking and planning ahead, trusting your instincts, making decisions to stay safe, looking out for the welfare of others, seeking help and guidance when you don't know the answers, and using plain old common sense, you are thinking like a leader.

Printed in the United States
by Baker & Taylor Publisher Services